All Kinds of Friends

My Friend Has Down Syndrome

by Kaitlyn Duling

Bullfrog
Books

Ideas for Parents and Teachers

Bullfrog Books let children practice reading informational text at the earliest reading levels. Repetition, familiar words, and photo labels support early readers.

Before Reading

• Discuss the cover photo. What does it tell them?

• Look at the picture glossary together. Read and discuss the words.

Read the Book

• "Walk" through the book and look at the photos. Let the child ask questions. Point out the photo labels.

• Read the book to the child, or have him or her read independently.

After Reading

• Prompt the child to think more. Ask: Do you know someone with Down syndrome? What do you like about him or her?

Bullfrog Books are published by Jump!
5357 Penn Avenue South
Minneapolis, MN 55419
www.jumplibrary.com

Copyright © 2020 Jump! International copyright reserved in all countries. No part of this book may be reproduced in any form without written permission from the publisher.

Library of Congress Cataloging-in-Publication Data

Names: Duling, Kaitlyn, author.
Title: My friend has Down syndrome / by Kaitlyn Duling.
Description: Minneapolis, MN: Jump!, Inc., 2020.
Series: All kinds of friends | Includes index.
Audience: Age 5–8. | Audience: K to Grade 3.
Identifiers: LCCN 2018052234 (print)
LCCN 2018055772 (ebook)
ISBN 9781641287289 (ebook)
ISBN 9781641287265 (hardcover : alk. paper)
ISBN 9781641287272 (pbk.)
Subjects: LCSH: Down syndrome—Juvenile literature.
Children with disabilities—Juvenile literature.
Friendship—Juvenile literature.
Classification: LCC RC571 (ebook)
LCC RC571 .D85 2019 (print) | DDC 616.85/8842—dc23
LC record available at https://lccn.loc.gov/2018052234

Editor: Susanne Bushman
Designer: Molly Ballanger

Photo Credits: Tad Saddoris, cover, 16–17 (foreground); FatCamera/iStock, 1; Monkey Business Images/Shutterstock, 3; SolStock/iStock, 4, 5, 6–7, 23tl; asiseeit/iStock, 8–9; DenKuvaiev/iStock, 10; kali9/iStock, 11, 14–15, 18, 19, 23br; Steve Debenport/iStock, 12–13, 23bl; cristovao/Shutterstock, 16–17 (background); Maskot/Getty, 20–21; Patrick Foto/Shutterstock, 22 (left); Valua Vitaly/Shutterstock, 22 (right); Tony Stock/Shutterstock, 23tr; wilpunt/iStock, 24.

Printed in the United States of America at Corporate Graphics in North Mankato, Minnesota.

Table of Contents

Fun with Friends

This is Ben.

He is my friend.

Ben is fun!

We love to play.

5

Ben has Down syndrome.
Some skills are easy
for him.

Others are hard.

Speaking can
be hard for Joy.

I listen closely.

She tells funny jokes!

Peg's muscles get tired.

She runs slowly.

**Exercise helps Liz.
It makes her stronger.**

helper

Ty and I learn a new skill.

He takes a little longer.

I am patient.

I help.

Jan notices Mom's feelings.
She knows when she is sad.
She makes her smile.

We help each other.

We are good friends.

Kim looks a little different from me.

We all look unique.
That is okay!

We are a lot alike.

Different Strengths

Everyone has different abilities. Some things are harder for us than they are for others.

Think about yourself. What is easy for you? What is hard? Do one thing that is easy for you. Then do one thing that is more difficult. You can ask a friend for help!

Finally, see if you can help a friend or family member do something that is hard for them. When we help each other, we all win.

Down syndrome
A condition that some people are born with that gives them special features, gifts, and challenges.

muscles
Tissues that are attached to your skeleton and pull on your bones to make them move.

patient
Able to accept delays or problems without getting angry or upset.

unique
Being one of a kind and unlike anyone else.

Index

To Learn More

FACT SURFER

Finding more information is as easy as 1, 2, 3.

❶ Go to www.factsurfer.com

❷ Enter "myfriendhasDownsyndrome" into the search box.

❸ Choose your book to see a list of websites.